THE (MOSTLY) COMPLETE POEMS OF ELIZABETH ELEANOR SIDDAL

This volume is # 402 / 1,862

*Elizabeth's manuscript for "Ope not thy lips, thou foolish one",
currently in the Ashmolean Museum at Oxford.*

THE
(MOSTLY)
COMPLETE POEMS OF ELIZABETH ELEANOR SIDDAL

WITH AN INTRODUCTION BY
KYLE CASSIDY

LAUREL TREE PRESS
PHILADELPHIA · SPITALFIELDS

Introduction & cover photograph
    © 2024 Kyle Cassidy / Trillian Stars
Cover design
    © 2024 Madeline Carol Matz — MCMatz.com
Poppy, thistle & rose illustrations
    © 2024 by Kambriel

Elizabeth's poems are in the public domain,
please share them with people who will enjoy them.

978-1-948886-48-2

Published by Laurel Tree Press

First Printing, August, 2024

October 6th. — Called on Dante Rossetti. Saw Miss Siddal, looking thinner and more deathlike and more beautiful and more ragged than ever; a real artist, a woman without parallel for many a long year. Gabriel as usual diffuse and inconsequent in his work. Drawing wonderful and lovely Guggums one after another, each one a fresh charm, each one stamped with immortality, and his picture never advancing.... Poor Gabriello. . . .

— Ford Madox Brown's diary

CONTENTS

INTRODUCTION 1

THE POEMS OF
ELIZABETH ELEANOR SIDDAL 13

OH GRIEVE NOT WITH THY
BITTER TEARS 15

RUTHLESS HANDS HAVE TORN HER
FROM ONE THAT LOVED HER WELL 16

O SILENT WOOD, I ENTER THEE 17

OPE NOT THY LIPS, THOU FOOLISH ONE 18

O GOD, FORGIVE ME THAT I MERGED
MY LIFE INTO A DREAM OF LOVE 20

LIFE AND NIGHT ARE
FALLING FROM ME 22

Farewell, Earl Richard
tender and brave 24

Never weep for love that's dead 26

Now Christ thee save,
thou bonny shepherd 27

To touch the glove upon
her tender hand 28

Many a mile o'er land and sea 29

I care not for My Lady's soul 30

Thy strong arms are
around me, love 31

Slow days have passed
that make a year 33

O mother, open the window
wide and let the daylight in 35

Letter to Dante Gabriel Rossetti 37

A note on the sources 40

Colophon 42

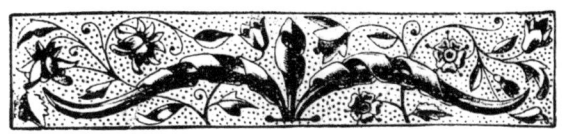

INTRODUCTION

Elizabeth Eleanor Siddal,
   aka Elizabeth Siddall,
   aka Elizabeth Eleanor Rossetti,
   aka Lizzie,
   aka Miss Sid,
   aka The Sid,
   aka Sids,
   aka Ida,
   aka Dove,
   aka Gug,
   aka Guggums

— 25 July 1829 - 11 February 1862

Elizabeth Siddal was a multifaceted creative — a Renaissance woman trapped in the long shadow of Queen Victoria. In the field of painting, she enjoyed considerable success, acquiring the patronage of England's foremost art critic, John Ruskin, who dubbed her *genius*, bought

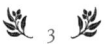

every single work at her first show, and paid her the staggering sum of £150 a year simply for the right of first refusal to purchase any art she produced. While painting was her vocation, she was also a skilled poet. She wrote, as inspiration struck, on scraps of paper and the backs of letters, but always revising and reworking.

At the age of 32, her life and plans were cut short by a laudanum overdose before she had a chance to publish, or even prepare for publication, any of her work. Her surviving poetic output is small, amounting to only about 15 poems and some unfinished stanzas, but it is remarkable in its power and honesty, lacking the forced hyperbolic subject matter of many of her peers.

In the months after her death, her husband, Dante Gabriel Rossetti, toyed with the idea of publishing her poetry as a memorial and suggested to his sister, the well-known poet, Christina Rossetti, that they might appear as a section in her forthcoming book *The Prince's Progress*. After reading Lizzie's oeuvre, Christina balked, deciding that they were "too hopelessly sad" and suggested that if Dante *really* wanted to publish them he should include them in an upcoming volume of *his* (he never did).

> "I think with you that, between your volume and mine, their due post of honour is in yours. But do you not think that (at any rate except in your volume), beautiful as they are, they are almost too hopelessly sad for publication en masse. Perhaps this is merely my overstrained fancy, but their tone is to me even painfully despondent ...."[1]

And thus, without a champion, Lizzie's poems entered into obscurity.

Christina (certainly no stranger to a somber verse) was always aloof *around* and never quite approved *of* Miss Sids. She believed her brother had an unhealthy cacoëthes with Lizzie — the two spent most of their time alone together, avoiding friends. In seclusion, Dante was continually and obsessively sketching his wife performing whatever task she was engaged in (reading, sleeping, painting, moving furniture, staring out of windows) ignoring his obligations and filling

---

[1] Christina Rossetti, letter to her brother, 10 Feb 1865. Rossetti, William Michael, Dante Gabriel Rossetti, and Christina Georgina Rossetti. *Rossetti Papers, 1862 to 1870: a Compilation by William Michael Rossetti.* New York: Scribner, 1903. p. 78

endless drawers with these doodles he called "Guggums" (a name they used, interchangeably, for one another).[2]

Apart from her husband and John Ruskin, one of her few close confidants was the poet Algernon Swinburne who wrote, after her death: "I never knew so brilliant and appreciative a woman — so quick to see and so keen to enjoy that rare and delightful fusion of wit, humour, character-painting, and dramatic poetry — poetry subdued to dramatic effect — which is only less wonderful and delightful than the highest works of genius." At another time Swinburne writes "To one at least who knew her better than most of her husband's friends, the memory of all her marvelous charms of mind and person — her matchless grace, loveliness, courage, endurance, wit, humor, heroism, and sweetness — is too dear and sacred to be profaned by any attempt at expression."[3]

---

2   While the "drawers" full of Guggums have been scattered to the wind, sold and given away over the years, a few reside in the Victoria and Albert Museum in London. The volume of them must have been considerable; multiple friends made note of them littering the apartment.

3   Both Swinburne quotes in Rossetti, Dante Gabriel, &

One may wonder if we would have known her more as a poet and less as a face if her husband had passed her notebooks off to Swinburne after her death. But as it is, her reputation was, at last, left to William Rossetti, family biographer and never a fan of Miss Sid, and who, like Christina, found her incomprehensible. "Her inner personality," he wrote, "did not float upon the surface of her speech or bearing; to me it remained, if not strictly enigmatic, still mainly undivulged."4

William, in his various family histories, seems to be trying from the depths of his heart to think of something nice to say about his sister-in-law but proves incapable. He will occasionally disgorge some faint praise but swiftly race to undermine it two sentences later in a fevered exuberance as though he fears it balancing too long unchecked in a reader's mind. And Elizabeth might not have cared much to win her brother-in-law's affection — as biographer Lucinda Hawksley says, "she

---

William Michael Rossetti. *Dante Gabriel Rossetti; His Family-Letters, with a Memoir by William Michael Rossetti.* Ellis & Elvey, 1895. p. 175

4 Rossetti, William Michael. *Some Reminiscences of William Michael Rossetti.* London: Brown, Langham, 1906. p. 193

could charm anyone she believed worth charming, and snub without compunction anyone she was not in the mood to entertain."[5] Few of her letters survive, and no diaries, so, we are left to glean her story from the most imperfect of biographers, interested at best in minimizing and at worst in vilifying her.[6] The examples we have of Elizabeth Siddal's poetry come from William's various biographies of his brother, published in three tranches. In the second, in 1899, he writes:

> I present here seven specimens of Miss Siddal's verse; an eighth was given in my Memoir of Dante Rossetti. She used to take a great deal of pains, and I fancy was seldom or never satisfied with her productions. One can find a dozen scribblings of the same stanza here and there, modified and corrected. As to the date of these poems I am not certain, but should suppose that her most productive years were from 1855 to 1857...[7]

---

5 Hawksley, Lucinda, *Lizzie Siddal: The Tragedy of a Pre-Raphaelite Supermodel,* Andre Deutsch, 2014, p. 16

6 The Sid's surviving letters are so demonstrative of her personality that we have included one in this volume.

7 Rossetti, William Michael. *Ruskin, Rossetti, Preraphaelitism: Papers 1854-1862*. London: G. Allen, 1899. p. 150

And then in the last, in 1906:

> ... There are in my hands some other slight scraps, scanty in every sense of the term. I consider that, from this time forward, no further verses by my sister-in-law remain of which the publication would be at all manageable. Those which I here reproduce do not bear any title in her own handwriting: I have thought it better to supply titles. I cannot speak to the dates of these compositions. My only criterion would be the handwriting (a matter in which Lizzie was never an adept); and, so far as I see, the handwriting of all the verses, with one exception, might belong either to her unmarried or to her wedded days. The exception is the final piece, called ["Life and night are falling from me"]. This is written in a very shaky and straggling way; I surmise that it must have been done under the influence of laudanum, which she frequently took by medical orders as a palliative against tormenting neuralgia, and probably not long before her death. There is a wail of pang and pathos in it not readily forgettable. Indeed, one of the most noticeable points in her verses generally (I will not say uniformly) is their excessive and seldom-relieved melancholy — a "darkness that can be felt." It is however a melancholy which to some extent merges into

a future hope the sense of settled desolation in this world. The verses give more evidence of a certain spiritual faith, pervasive though undefined, than I ever heard in the writer's conversation. [8, 9]

From this we may infer that the amount of papers handed over to him must have been significantly more substantial than what he printed. Many (some? all? a few?) of them exist now in the Ashmolean Museum at Oxford. A sixteenth poem, "Autumnal Leaves Have Fallen", was "discovered" and printed in 1978 in Roger C. Lewis & Mark Samuels Lasner's *Poems and Drawings of Elizabeth Siddal*. I have chosen not to include it here because its provenance is dubious and it appears to be a fragment anyway.

Miss Sid's poems have remained obscure since the time they were written. There have been occasional

---

8 Rossetti, William Michael. *Some Reminiscences of William Michael Rossetti*. London: Brown, Langham, 1906. pp. 195-196.

9 It's also worth noting that William Rossetti continually refers to her as "Miss Siddal" rather than by her married name "Mrs. Rossetti". We may assume either he was a feminist far ahead of his time, or that he believed her not quite worthy of the family name.

publications of some of them, both on-line and in various books, most of which have extremely inconsistent line spacings, punctuation and indentation.

William Rossetti did a significant amount of editing to Elizabeth's poems before printing them, and it is far beyond the scope of this book to attempt to unwind or evaluate those changes. I've left intact his formatting and word choices (even when I believe his decipherment of her handwriting, of which he complained bitterly, is incorrect) but I have removed his (often intrusive, often overwrought, often oblivious) titles and substituted first lines.

As much as I do not trust William Rossetti, his edits are at least accurate to the period. It is often difficult to glean Elizabeth's intent or how her work would have been formatted upon publication or had she the opportunity to make fair copies.

The authoritative academic edition of Elizabeth's work is certainly 2018's *My Ladys Soul* by Dr. Serena Trowbridge who examines and tries to reconcile the multiple versions of poems, scraps and ephemera Elizabeth left behind and undo some of the damage of prior printings, though she does not speculate as to what a Victorian editor would have done with the formatting.

I've also chosen to spell her name *Siddal* instead of *Siddall* (her birth name.) She signed letters both ways, but I'll err on the side of a pen-name she chose rather than one she inherited. (There are loud, late-night arguments in favor of each, taking place in hotel bars at academic conferences every year— if you're a few martinis in and looking to start a fight with some English Lit professors, this is an excellent place to begin.)

— *Kyle Cassidy, London, December 2023*

OH GRIEVE NOT WITH THY BITTER TEARS

Oh grieve not with thy bitter tears
    The life that passes fast:
The gates of heaven will open wide,
    And take me in at last.

Then sit down meekly at my side,
    And watch my young life flee:
Then solemn peace of holy death
    Come quickly unto thee.

But, true love, seek me in the throng
    Of spirits floating past;
And I will take thee by the hands,
    And know thee mine at last.

RUTHLESS HANDS HAVE TORN HER FROM ONE THAT LOVED HER WELL

Ruthless hands have torn her
    From one that loved her well;
Angels have upborne her,
    Christ her grief to tell.

She shall stand to listen,
    She shall stand and sing,
Till three winged angels
    Her lover's soul shall bring.

He and she and the angels three
    Before God's face shall stand:
There they shall pray among themselves,
    And sing at His right hand.

O SILENT WOOD, I ENTER THEE

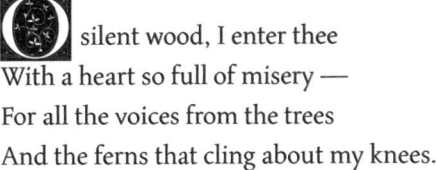O silent wood, I enter thee
With a heart so full of misery —
For all the voices from the trees
And the ferns that cling about my knees.

In thy darkest shadow let me sit
When the grey owls about thee flit:
There I will ask of thee a boon,
That I may not faint or die or swoon.

Gazing through the gloom like one
Whose life and hopes are also done,
Frozen like a thing of stone,
I sit in thy shadow — but not alone.

Can God bring back the day when we two stood
Beneath the clinging trees in that dark wood?

OPE NOT THY LIPS, THOU FOOLISH ONE

Ope not thy lips, thou foolish one,
    Nor turn to me thy face:
The blasts of heaven shall strike me down
    Ere I will give thee grace.

Take thou thy shadow from my path,
    Nor turn to me and pray:
The wild, wild winds thy dirge may sing
    Ere I will bid thee stay.

Lift up thy false brow from the dust,
    Nor wild thine hands entwine
Among the golden summer-leaves
    To mock the gay sunshine.

And turn away thy false dark eyes,
    Nor gaze into my face:
Great love I bore thee; now great hate
    Sits grimly in its place.

All changes pass me like a dream,
    I neither sing nor pray;
And thou art like the poisonous tree
    That stole my life away.

O GOD, FORGIVE ME THAT I MERGED[†] MY LIFE INTO A DREAM OF LOVE

O God, forgive me that I merged
    My life into a dream of love!
Will tears of anguish never wash
    The poison from my blood?

Love kept my heart in a song of joy,
    My pulses quivered to the tune;
The coldest blasts of winter blew
    Upon me like sweet airs in June.

Love floated on the mists of morn,
    And rested on the sunset's rays;
He calmed the thunder of the storm,
    And lighted all my ways.

Love held me joyful through the day,
    And dreaming ever through the night:
No evil thing could come to me,
    My spirit was so light.

Oh Heaven help my foolish heart
    Which heeded not the passing time
That dragged my idol from its place
    And shattered all its shrine!

†   Note: The word in Elizabeth's original manuscript, while difficult to decipher, is definitely not "merged". Over the years some scholars have read it as "ranged", a word which, although now obsolete, Tennyson uses in *Idylls of the King* to mean systematically ordered or arranged.

LIFE AND NIGHT ARE FALLING FROM ME

Life and night are falling from me,
Death and day are opening on me.
Wherever my footsteps come and go
Life is a stony way of woe.
    Lord, have I long to go?
Hollow hearts are ever near me,
Soulless eyes have ceased to cheer me:
    Lord, may I come to Thee?
Life and youth and summer weather
To my heart no joy can gather:
Lord, lift me from life's stony way.
Loved eyes, long closed in death, watch o'er me —
Holy Death is waiting for me —
    Lord, may I come to-day?

My outward life feels sad and still,
Like lilies in a frozen rill.
I am gazing upwards to the sun,
Lord, Lord, remembering my lost one.
    O Lord, remember me!
How is it in the unknown land?
Do the dead wander hand in hand?
Do we clasp dead hands, and quiver
With an endless joy for ever?
Is the air filled with the sound
Of spirits circling round and round?
Are there lakes, of endless song,
To rest our tirèd eyes upon?
Do tall white angels gaze and wend
Along the banks where lilies bend?
Lord, we know not how this may be;
Good Lord, we put our faith in Thee —
    O God, remember me.

FAREWELL, EARL RICHARD
TENDER AND BRAVE

Farewell, Earl Richard,
    Tender and brave;
Kneeling I kiss
    The dust from thy grave.

Pray for me, Richard,
    Lying alone,
With hands pleading earnestly,
    All in white stone.

Soon must I leave thee
    This sweet summer tide;
That other is waiting
    To claim his pale bride.

Soon I'll return to thee.
    Hopeful and brave,
When the dead leaves
    Blow over thy grave.

Then shall they find me
    Close at thy head,
Watching or fainting,
    Sleeping or dead.

NEVER WEEP FOR LOVE THAT'S DEAD

Oh never weep for love that's dead,
    Since love is seldom true,
But changes his fashion from blue to red,
    From brightest red to blue,
And love was born to an early death
    And is so seldom true.

Then harbour no smile on your loving face
    To win the deepest sigh;
The fairest words on truest lips
    Pass off and surely die;
And you will stand alone, my dear,
    When wintry winds draw nigh.

Sweet, never weep for what cannot be,
    For this God has not given:
If the merest dream of love were true,
    Then, sweet, we should be in heaven;
And this is only earth, my dear,
    Where true love is not given.

NOW CHRIST THEE SAVE, THOU BONNY SHEPHERD

Now Christ thee save, thou bonny Shepherd,
    Sailing on the sea;
Ten thousand souls are sailing there
    But I belong to thee.
If thou art lost then all is lost
    And all is dead to me.

My love should have a grey head-stone
    And green moss at his feet,
And clinging grass above his breast
    Whereon his lambs could bleat;
And I should know the span of earth
    Where one day I might sleep.

TO TOUCH THE GLOVE UPON
HER TENDER HAND

To touch the glove upon her tender hand,
    To watch the jewel sparkle in her ring,
Lifted my heart into a sudden song,
    As when the wild birds sing.

To track her shadow on the sunny grass,
    To break her pathway through the darkened wood,
Filled all my life with trembling and tears
    And silence where I stood.

I watch the shadows gather round my heart,
    I live to know that she is gone —
Gone, gone for ever, like the tender dove
    That left the ark alone.

MANY A MILE O'ER LAND AND SEA

Many a mile o'er land and sea
Unsummoned my Love returned to me;
I remember not the words he said,
But only the trees mourning overhead.
And he came ready to take and bear
The cross I had carried for many a year:
But my words came slowly one by one
From frozen lips that were still and dumb.
How sounded my words so still and slow
To the great strong heart that loved me so?
Ah I remember, my God, so well,
How my brain lay dumb in a frozen spell;
And I leaned away from my lover's face
To watch the dead leaves that were running a race.
I felt the spell that held my breath,
Bending me down to a living death —
As if hope lay buried when he had come
Who knew my sorrows all and some.

I CARE NOT FOR MY LADY'S SOUL

I care not for my Lady's soul,
    Though I worship before her smile:
I care not where be my Lady's goal
    When her beauty shall lose its wile.

Low sit I down at my Lady's feet.
    Gazing through her wild eyes,
Smiling to think how my love will fleet
    When their starlike beauty dies.

I care not if my Lady pray
    To our Father which is in Heaven;
But for joy my heart's quick pulses play,
    For to me her love is given.

Then who shall close my Lady's eyes,
    And who shall fold her hands?
Will any hearken if she cries
    Up to the unknown lands?

THY STRONG ARMS ARE AROUND ME, LOVE

Thy strong arms are around me, love,
    My head is on thy breast:
Though words of comfort come from thee,
    My soul is not at rest:

For I am but a startled thing,
    Nor can I ever be
Aught save a bird whose broken wing
    Must fly away from thee.

I cannot give to thee the love
    I gave so long ago —
The love that turned and struck me down
    Amid the blinding snow.

I can but give a sinking heart
    And weary eyes of pain,
A faded mouth that cannot smile
    And may not laugh again.

Yet keep thine arms around me, love,
    Until I drop to sleep:
Then leave me — saying no good-bye,
    Lest I might fall and weep.

SLOW DAYS HAVE PASSED THAT MAKE A YEAR

Slow days have passed that make a year,
    Slow hours that make a day,
Since I could take my first dear love,
    And kiss him the old way:
Yet the green leaves touch me on the cheek,
    Dear Christ, this month of May.

I lie among the tall green grass
    That bends above my head,
And covers up my wasted face,
    And folds me in its bed
Tenderly and lovingly
    Like grass above the dead.

Dim phantoms of an unknown ill
    Float through my tiring brain;
The unformed visions of my life
    Pass by in ghostly train;
Some pause to touch me on the cheek,
    Some scatter tears like rain.

The river ever running down
    Between its grassy bed,
The voices of a thousand birds
    That clang above my head,
Shall bring to me a sadder dream
    When this sad dream is dead.

A silence falls upon my heart,
    And hushes all its pain.
I stretch my hands in the long grass,
    And fall to sleep again,
There to lie empty of all love,
    Like beaten corn of grain.

O MOTHER, OPEN THE WINDOW WIDE AND LET THE DAYLIGHT IN

O mother, open the window wide
    And let the daylight in;
The hills grow darker to my sight,
    And thoughts begin to swim.

And mother dear, take my young son
    (Since I was born of thee),
And care for all his little ways,
    And nurse him on thy knee.

And, mother, wash my pale, pale hands,
    And then bind up my feet;
My body may no longer rest
    Out of its winding-sheet.

And, mother dear, take a sapling twig
    And green grass newly mown,
And lay them on my empty bed,
    That my sorrow be not known.

And mother, find three berries red
    And pluck them from the stalk,
And burn them at the first cockcrow,
    That my spirit may not walk.

And, mother dear, break a willow wand,
    And if the sap be even,
Then save it for my lover's sake,
    And he'll know my soul's in heaven.

And, mother, when the big tears fall
    (And fall, God knows, they may),
Tell him I died of my great love,
    And my dying heart was gay.

And mother dear, when the sun has set,
    And the pale kirk grass waves,
Then carry me through the dim twilight
    And hide me among the graves.

LETTER TO DANTE GABRIEL ROSSETTI — NICE, FRANCE, CHRISTMAS-TIME 1855

[Note: the beginning of this letter is lost.]

On your leaving the boat, your passport is taken from you to the Police Station, and there taken charge of till you leave Nice. If a letter is sent to you containing money, the letter is detained at the Post Office, and another written to you by the postmaster ordering you to present yourself and passport for his inspection. You have then to go to the Police Station and beg the loan of your passport for half-an-hour, and are again looked upon as a felon of the first order before passport is returned to you. Looking very much like a transport, you make your way to the Post Office, and there present yourself before a grating, which makes the man behind it look like an overdone mutton-chop sticking to a gridiron. On asking for a letter containing money, Mutton-chop sees at once that you are a murderer, and makes up its mind not to let you off alive; and, treating you as Cain and Alice Gray[1] in one, demands your passport. After glaring at this and your face (which by this time becomes scarlet, and is taken at once as a token of guilt), a book is pushed through the bars of gridiron, and you are expected to sign your death-warrant by writing something which does not answer to the writing on the passport. Meanwhile Mutton-chop has been looking as much like doom as overdone mutton can look, fizzing in French, not one word of which is understood by Alice Gray. But now comes the reward of merit. Mutton sees at once that no two people living and at large could write so badly as the writing on the passport and that in the book; so takes me for Alice, but gives me the money, and wonders whether I shall be let off from hard labour the next time I am taken, on account of my thinness. When you enter the Police Station to return the passport. You are glared at through wooden bars

---

1   "Alice Gray" was one of the many aliases of Mary Atkinson (aka: *Miss Hook, Alice Christie, Eliza Tremaine, Anastasia Carter, Anastasia Huggard, etc., etc.*) known by the press as "The Imposter" a one-woman crime wave fascinating and terrorizing England in the latter half of 1855, mostly scamming people out of money. She was apprehended and went on trial in November, charged with 30 different crimes.

with marked surprise at not returning in company of two cocked-hats, and your fainting look is put down to your having been found out in something. They are forced, however, to content themselves by expecting to have a job in a day or so. This is really what one has to put up with, and its not at all comic when one is ill. I will write again when boil[2] is better, or tell you about lodgings if we are able to get any. There was an English dinner here on Christmas Day, ending with plum-pudding, which was really very good indeed, and an honour to the country. I dined up in my room, where I have dined for the last three weeks on account of bores. First class, one can get to the end of the world; but one can never be let alone or left at rest.

But believe me
    Yours most affectionately,
        Lizzy

---

2   Rossetti aparantly shared this letter with John Ruskin who wrote back "Many a boil-over have I had by myself at the passport system…"

A NOTE ON THE SOURCES

The poems of Elizabeth Siddal collected in this volume can be found in:

Rossetti, William Michael. *Ruskin, Rossetti, Preraphaelitism: Papers 1854-1862.* London: G. Allen, 1899 pp. 150-156

"O mother, open the window wide"
"Farewell, Earl Richard, tender and brave"
"Oh never weep for a love that's dead"
"Now Christ thee save, thou bonny Shepherd"
"To touch the glove upon her tender hand"
"Many a mile o'er land and sea"
"I care not for my Lady's soul"
"Thy strong arms are around me, love"
"Letter to Dante Gabriel Rossetti" (p. 112)

Rossetti, Dante Gabriel & Rossetti, William Michael. *Dante Gabriel Rossetti; His Family-Letters, with a Memoir* by *William Michael Rossetti*. Ellis and Elvey, 1895 pp. 176-177

"Slow days have passed that make a year".

Rossetti, William Michael. *Some Reminiscences of William Michael Rossetti*. London: Brown, Langham, 1906 pp. 196-200

"Oh grieve not with thy bitter tears"
"Ruthless hands have torn her …"
"Oh silent wood, I enter thee"
"Ope not thy lips, thou foolish one"
"Oh God forgive me that I merged my life…"
"Life and night are falling from me"

William also published "Oh Silent Wood, I enter thee" in *The Burlington Magazine for Connoisseurs*, May 1903, Vol. 1. No. 3, pp 291-292 with slightly different punctuation plus one of Elizabeth's self-portraits and five Guggums by her husband.

COLOPHON

First
printing limited to
1,862 copies, numbered 1 through
1,862, with 20 additional copies, lettered A
through T, reserved for the publisher. ¶ This book
was published in conjunction with *This is Only Earth,
My Dear: Images by Trillian Stars & Kyle Cassidy With Poems
by Elizabeth Eleanor Siddal* ¶ *(ISBN: 978-1-948886-47-5)*. ¶ Designed by Kyle Cassidy. ¶ This book is set in Maiola by Veronika
Burian from TypeTogether. Maiola is a readable contemporary
typeface which relies on humanist and calligraphic features. It
was released in 2005. The Initial Caps are Fleur Corner Caps by
Merethe Liljedahl. The typographic ornaments are copied from
the 1882 Hurst & Co. publication of the *Poems of Edgar Allan
Poe*. ¶ First Printing, August 2024. ¶ Published by Laurel
Tree Press, a division of Laurel Tree Theater; producing
works by, about, and benefiting women.
JenniferSummerfield.com
ElizabethSiddal.com
KyleCassidy.com

1862: Elizabeth Siddal's London

1) #7 Greville (Charles) Street, Elizabeth's childhood ho[me]
2) #3 Cranbourne Street, Mary Tozer's hat shop.
3) #14 Chatham Place, Blackfriars, married home & plac[e] of Elizabeth's death.
4) #4 Russell Place, Fitzroy Square, 1st art exhibition.